SCOTTISH
Clans & Tartans

Text by
Alastair Cunningham

Colin Baxter Photography Ltd, Grantown-on-Spey, Scotland

CLANS

For some people the clan system may seem a vague concept, associated perhaps with colourful tartans and tragic battles, and in particular with the defeat of Prince Charles Edward and his gallant Highland army at Culloden in 1746. But it was the clan system that provided the economic and social structure of the Highlands for about five hundred years and for those of Highland descent, their clan is a worldwide family, engendering pride in their background and a unique sense of belonging.

Origin of the Clans

The story begins in about 500 BC with restless Celtic tribes from east central Europe arriving in Britain. We know them from their distinctive art and design, but not from any written records, since their history was preserved only in the songs and tales of their bards. This was a warrior race: fighting was not just for survival but also for sport and, like later game sportsmen in the Scottish Highlands, they preserved their victims' heads as trophies to show off to visitors. These invaders of Britain were in turn conquered by Angles and Saxons who seized the heart of Britain, and it was only in the west and north of the island that Celtic culture survived.

Scots, Picts and Britons were the dominant tribes in North Britain, when in AD 843, the land north of the rivers Forth and Clyde was united as the Kingdom of Scotland. The ethnic composition and the boundaries of the new kingdom changed many times over the next two hundred years, but the centre of power always remained in the Highlands and the language of the court was that now known as Gaelic.

This changed in the reign of King Malcolm III '*ceann mor*', big head, (1058 - 1093). He married the Saxon Princess Margaret Atheling and during his reign Anglo-Saxon replaced Gaelic as the principal language of the court which was also moved to Dunfermline near the Firth of Forth. Three of Margaret's sons became kings in their turn. The last, David I (1084-1153), established his capital even further south, in Edinburgh and brought with him from the English court where he was raised, a number of educated and accomplished Norman and Flemish friends.

By the 12th century Highlanders found themselves remote from the law-giver. The old structure of provincial earls, who had previously administered justice, had collapsed and raids from neighbouring glens on cattle, the clansmen's principal

Murray

The name Murray is from the Celtic kingdom of Moray and was taken by a Flemish knight given lands there by King David I. Murrays have made their mark on Scottish history. It was Sir Andrew Murray, not William Wallace, who first led the struggle for Scottish independence – but he fell at the Battle of Stirling Bridge. Sir George Murray would later be Prince Charles Edward's most skilled general. The clan heartland is in Perthshire and since 1703 the Murray Chiefs have been Dukes of Atholl, whose seat is Blair Castle.

On a promontory by Loch Ness, (opposite) Urquhart was a strategic castle for successive Kings of Scots, controlling traffic through the Great Glen.

Each autumn thousands of cattle were driven through bleak Glen Lyon en route to markets in the south. This was also land where the expansionist Campbells confronted Stewarts and Murrays.

wealth, were commonplace. In the absence of any other form of law enforcement, they created their own system. Highland geography, with its natural frontiers of mountain ranges, lochs and the sea itself, provided identifiable homelands which could conveniently be dominated by a strong leader. The Celtic tradition of a strong kinship group, with a warrior Chief taking responsibility for the tribe's welfare, provided a natural social structure.

At least for the next four hundred years, these Celtic peoples had come to the end of their wanderings; clan lands evolved like a cluster of mini states with the Chief as land-holder, law-giver, judge and leader in battle. Geography and history had combined to retain an ancient culture in something of a pastoral time warp.

Highlands and Lowlands grew ever further apart. Indeed, to the (largely Anglo-Saxon) inhabitants of the Scottish capital, the Highlands were like a foreign country peopled by a different race, speaking a different language, wearing different dress. As Dr Samuel Johnson remarked as late as 1773, 'To the southern inhabitants of Scotland, the state of the mountains and the islands is equally known with that of Borneo or Sumatra: of both they have heard little and guess the rest.'

THE GAELIC LANGUAGE

The Scots brought Gaelic from Ireland around the 5th century and it slowly became commonplace throughout most of Scotland, even at the crowning of Scottish kings. However, in the 11th century it was replaced by Anglo-Saxon as the court language and fell into a decline. Its cause was not helped by its close association with the rebellious Highland clans; indeed in 1609 clan Chiefs were forced by statute to have their eldest sons taught English. Given the threat of extinction, Gaelic is now used as a teaching medium in primary schools and is readily accessible on radio and TV. About 60,000 people now speak it.

Kilchurn Castle on Loch Awe was built by the Campbells of Glenorchy, notably the 16th-century property magnate 'Black Duncan of the Seven Castles'.

MacLean (Modern)

Clan Identity

The oral tradition of bards played an important role in early clan identity. The noble and heroic origin of a clan, real or imagined, was fundamental and tales were told of descent from notable Celtic warriors. The name of Gillean of the Battleaxe still resonates well for MacLeans. The MacDougall and MacDonald bards had a similarly good story, being descended from the Norse-Celtic Somerled (c1126-64), the self-styled king and ruler of the west coast of Scotland in the twelfth century. MacGregors, MacKinnons, MacKays, MacDuffs, MacMillans, MacNabs and Robertsons all claim royal Scottish descent, whilst MacLachlans and MacNeils trace their ancestry to Niall of the Nine Hostages, the fifth-century king of Ulster. The Campbells claim not just Somerled but a great hero from Celtic mythology, Diarmaid the Boar,

and so call themselves Clan Diarmaid. The Rollo bards have a particularly long tale – once Norse Earls of Shetland, then settlers in Normandy, next as invaders of England with William the Conqueror, and arriving back in Scotland with King David I.

Not all King David's companions had such a long pedigree as the Rollos, some of them, like Robert de Brus, William de Comyn and William de Graham, would found dynasties with descendants who became new heroes that were just as Scottish as the sons of Somerled: Robert the Bruce as king, William Comyn as a would-be king, and James Graham, Marquis of Montrose as one of Scotland's greatest generals.

The word 'clan' is from the Gaelic *clann*, children, and a strong bond of kinship has always been fundamental in Celtic society. But it is misleading to imagine that all clan members were related. In our present (post-warrior) society, clan members are united by a common surname. However it is only in the last three hundred years that surnames have become commonly used in Scotland. Before that, nicknames or patronymics such as *Dhomnuil mac Challum*, Donald son of Malcolm, were quite sufficient in a small community.

If required to provide a surname, most Highlanders would automatically take that of their Chief, thus prudently signifying their allegiance. A literate person such as the minister might even have made this seemingly inconsequential decision on their behalf. In the early eighteenth century a number of MacRaes came over from the west coast to Beauly looking for work, and on being given a measure of meal happily took the name Fraser; they are still referred to as the 'boll-of-meal Frasers'. So it was that clans like the Gordons and Frasers, founded by individual Norman knights,

who were granted land in the Highlands by royal charter in the fourteenth century could, despite costly battles in the interim, produce armies numbered in thousands just three hundred years later. Conversely, the MacDougalls, descended from Somerled's eldest son Ranald, were once powerful enough to take on Robert the Bruce's army, but notably failed to win an encounter at the Pass of Brander in 1309, and are now not so numerous.

THE SENNACHIE

The sennachie held an exalted position in the clan hierarchy. He was the custodian of the clan history recounting, at some length, the Chief's pedigree. He also celebrated the heroic exploits of his ancestors and exhorted the Chief to follow their noble example. These morale-boosting speeches were given not just at the Chief's table but also on the field of battle where the disgrace associated with cowardly retreat was also given a good airing.

The River Avon rises in the Cairngorm mountains and flows through the fertile lands of Clan Grant, joining the Spey at Ballindalloch Castle.

Cameron (Modern)

Had 'Gentle Lochiel' the Cameron Chief, not supported Prince Charles Edward, the 1745 Rising would probably have been a flash in the pan. However Lochiel came from a dynasty of warrior Chiefs, who were traditional supporters of the Stewarts from their lands near Fort William. Against his better judgement he gave the lead, but eventually followed his Prince into exile where he died of wounds received at the Battle of Culloden. His castle at Achnacarry was burnt by government troops but has been rebuilt and is home to the present Lochiel.

MacDonald (Dress)

Somerled, Lord of the Isles, whose grandson Donald of Islay is the name ancestor of the MacDonalds, controlled the western seaboard and the islands in the mid 1150s. From then until the late 15th century, MacDonalds would repeatedly challenge the power of the Kings of Scots, attacking the king's castle at Urquhart on Loch Ness, disputing titles, and sacking Inverness. James IV finally invaded the islands and stripped MacDonald of his title, granting the various clan branches – Clanranald, Sleat, Keppoch and Glengarry – individual charters to their lands and so dissipating the previous centralised power.

Hierarchy and Customs

The relationship between a clansman and his Chief was not, as in England, one of nobleman and serf. General Wade remarked in 1724 that clansmen "are treated by their Chiefs with great familiarity. They partake with them in their diversions and shake them by the hand wherever they meet them". Many people observe that this classless mutual respect persists in much of rural Scotland today.

The Chief managed many clan affairs through men of his own kin called 'tacksmen' who played an important military and social role. They were leaseholders of land who sublet farming in 'clachans' (small villages) of eight or so families. They would also act as officers when military action was required and would call out the clan. For this they used the traditional 'fiery cross' – a wooden cross, burning or burnt, with a blood soaked rag attached – that was passed from hand to hand. This call-out system was successfully used in Canada in the winter of 1812/13 by the Glengarry Highlanders to repel an American raid!

The Chief was the father of his people and had personal responsibility for dispensing justice, for clan prosperity and all military decisions. The succession of a Chief with such enormous power could not be left to the lottery of primogeniture. Under a Celtic system known as 'tanistry' the Chief appointed one of his sons or nephews, or any other offspring of his great grandfather, as the next Chief, or Tanist. This pragmatic system effectively weeded out the mad, the bad and the simply unsuitable from the succession.

Another curious but effective practice was that of fostering. The children of the Chief and others of high status were routinely fostered out to the families of

Castle Stalker, a massive and simple keep on Loch Linnhe was built by Duncan Stewart of Appin and served as a hunting lodge for Kings of Scots.

Glencoe has passed into history due to the massacre of the MacDonalds in 1692, but this bleak and impressive glen is also notable as a mountaineering centre and for its extraordinary geology.

tacksmen; and tacksmen's children were fostered by those of higher rank. This created a web of close family ties that cut across the traditional hierarchy.

Alliances with other clans were vital, and tactical marriages proved a useful tool. Here again, success was not left to chance. Under the system of 'handfasting', the chosen couple lived together for one year and one day; if by then a child was born or expected, then the marriage was confirmed, if not, then both were free to handfast elsewhere.

Such diplomatic alliances were, as ever, backed by might: the Celtic warrior was never far from the surface. The clansman's main tasks were to mind hardy black cattle and grow some oats and barley; however the larger clans also boasted a warrior elite, too good for menial tasks, whose time was spent cattle raiding, hunting and patrolling the clan boundaries.

Cattle Droving

Small black cattle were the Highlander's principal wealth – but only theoretically until they were driven south to markets in Crieff, Falkirk and Carlisle. If he lived on Skye the beasts swam over the narrows to Glenelg; from the Western Isles they came by boat. In any case they travelled for weeks along traditional routes in the care of drovers and their dogs. In the remote glens, the drover would make a small fire, eat a handful of oatmeal mixed with boiling water, and lie down in the heather. Later, his charges joined a swell of other beasts on well used 'drove roads' through passes like Drumochter, north of Blair Atholl. Now life became a more sociable affair with strategic drovers' inns to rest in. But there was always the threat of 'black mail', the rent that had to be paid to clans en route to ensure that no black cattle disappeared overnight. Droving declined following the arrival of the railways in the late nineteenth century.

Clan Chiefs and Kings of Scots

Writing in 1720, an Officer posted to the Highlands wrote to a friend in London, 'The ordinary Highlanders esteem it the most sublime degree of virtue to love their Chief and pay him a blind obedience even though it be in opposition to the Government.' It was true. And in the Highland glens a man with no clan was dangerously exposed, lacking effective legal or military protection. Such an elegantly self-perpetuating system was a problem in the reign of successive Kings of Scots who could not appeal to the loyalty of any Highlander except through his Chief.

The actual powers of the Chiefs were legitimised by the king in two ways. He appointed them as 'hereditary Justiciars' in their region, with sentencing powers (including the death penalty); and he granted them parchment charters for their lands – contemptuously known by some as 'sheepskin grants'. The land charter was of course a double edged sword: what the king gave, he could also take away. And this feudal system also presented a conflict of interests, for the clansmen believed their clan land was held in trust for the clan, not by the Chief as owner. In the late eighteenth century many clansmen would become painfully aware of this significant legal detail.

The king's authority in international events was generally respected and the clans mustered when required to defend Scotland – at Bannockburn and Flodden for example (although the MacDonalds probably considered themselves to be the king's allies in such encounters). The king was the ultimate arbiter in inter-clan matters, but to enforce his will, he had to use other clans – ideally those who might already hold a grudge against the miscreant. The most prominent of the 'enforcing' clans were the Campbells of Argyll in the south west and the Gordons in the North East; neither of which was shy about annexing some territory as a just reward.

Another favoured tactic of Scottish kings was to place strong-arm kinsmen or friends in the Highlands, and grant them the lands of defeated or weakened clans. This was not always successful as many of these 'placemen', or their descendants, 'went native'. The descendants of the Norman knight de Frèzelière, for example, were universally known by the Gaelic patronymic *MacShimidh*, son of Simon, but after only three generations as Frasers of Lovat. However, the most notorious placeman was probably King Robert II's son Alexander Stewart, who was created Justiciar of the Northern Lowlands, Earl of Buchan, and granted lands in Badenoch and Strathspey. Later known as the 'Wolf of Badenoch', he became a ruthless tyrant, and when the Bishop of Moray was so bold as to criticise his domestic arrangements he rode to Elgin with a team of his ruffians and burnt down both town and cathedral. The Stewarts of Atholl are amongst his many descendants.

Glencoe

The Massacre of Glencoe is famous for both its brutality and its shameful breach of the Highland ethic of hospitality. William III, who seized the thrones of England and Scotland in 1688, had good reason to doubt the Highland Chiefs' allegiance and demanded that each sign a pledge of allegiance by 31 December 1691. Most signed in good time, but the recalcitrant Chief of the MacDonalds of Glencoe, for various reasons, only signed on 5 January. The government saw a chance to demonstrate its authority. So, on 1 February 1692 two companies, commanded by a Campbell, asked the MacDonalds for quarters in snowy Glencoe. They enjoyed Macdonald hospitality for twelve days, then orders came that their hosts should be slaughtered early the next morning. The Chief and his wife were amongst the 38 killed but his sons escaped. Many who fled up into the snow-filled corries will also have perished.

This family came to Scotland with David I in the 12th century. Always at the forefront of battle in the Wars of Independence, their most famous commander was the Marquis of Montrose who fought for Charles I.

Graham (Modern)

Massacre of Glencoe, by James Hamilton, painted in 1883/6. Despite an outcry throughout Scotland in 1692, no one was punished for the deed.

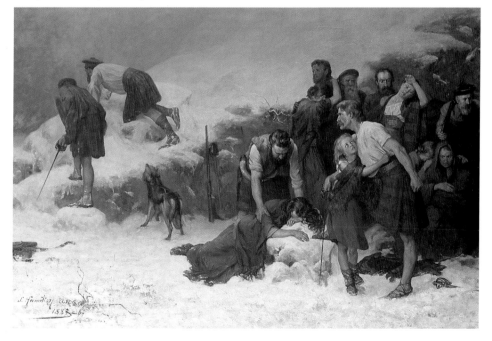

The Jacobites, the Battle of Culloden and its Aftermath

The Highlander's loyalty to his Chief was fundamental. And this may explain why so many clans supported the Jacobite cause which aimed to restore the exiled Stewart kings, the Chief of Chiefs, to regain their crown. The Stewarts were kings of Scots before also becoming kings of England and many Chiefs were unhappy with the removal of the Roman Catholic King James VII and II in favour of his Protestant nephew William III.

There were armed uprisings in favour of the exiled Stewarts in 1689, 1715, 1719 and in 1745. The principal supporters in each case were Highland clans. The Highland Charge was a significant weapon of war in the eighteenth century; an assault by wild, apparently fearless clansmen, swords aloft, charging to the strains of the pipes and screaming their war-cries in derision, was the stuff of nightmares for press-ganged recruits of the opposing army. This also reinforced the impression of Highlanders as warlike savages.

However, some clans like the Campbells, Mackays, Sutherlands, Grants, Brodies and Munros consistently supported the government. Others – MacKintoshes and Atholl Murrays – on occasions had men fighting on both sides. In the 1745 rising the Fraser Chief stayed at home whilst many of his clansmen fought in the front line under Fraser of Inverallochy.

The final Jacobite battle was on April 16th 1746 at Culloden, just outside Inverness, where Prince Charles Edward Stewart was defeated by his cousin the

Culloden Battlefield near Inverness, where the last Jacobite rising was decisively and brutally suppressed.

MacDuff (Mod. Hunting)

Clan Duff stems from Queen Gruoch, wife of MacBeth, and thereby from the original Royal Scoto-Pictish line. The Chiefs were Earls of Fife and as head of the senior clan, held the privilege of enthroning Scottish kings. However their power declined when the 12th Earl supported Edward I of England, his uncle by marriage, against Robert the Bruce, and the original line later died out. MacDuff Chiefs once held sway over most of eastern Scotland but the clan is principally associated with Fife and Aberdeenshire.

The monument at Glenfinnan by Loch Shiel (opposite), where Prince Charles Edward 'raised his standard' in 1745 signifying a rallying point for his followers. Few appeared until the pipes of the Cameron men were heard approaching.

The Battle of Culloden 16 April 1746 (above). A tired and hungry Jacobite army was outnumbered, outgunned and outmanoeuvred by government troops. Prince Charles Edward (opposite), grandson of the exiled King James II and VII: charismatic, charming, handsome, but no general.

Duke of Cumberland. It was an uneven encounter and its killing and burning aftermath gave an uncompromising signal of the government's determination to pluck the heart from Celtic Scotland and put a stop for ever to Highland-based rebellions. Shortly thereafter the hereditary powers of the Chiefs as 'Justiciars' were removed and the Act of Proscription (1746) banned the carrying of weapons, the wearing of Highland dress and the playing of bagpipes. There were no more risings, but the troubles of the Highlands were not over.

Clan Chiefs who had risen in 1745 were convicted of treason and their lands were forfeited to the government who sold them on. The new landlords wanted ground on which to graze their sheep; they had no use for fine warriors who could not pay a rent. In many cases clansmen, who had no rights, were simply evicted and made their way to the big cities or emigrated to North America. And the

The Jacobites

No presentation of Scottish history can avoid the word Jacobite! It comes from the latin *Jacobus* meaning James and refers to James VII and II Stewart king of both Scotland and England, whose nephew, William of Orange, invaded England in 1688. James fled to France and his family remained in exile thereafter, continually proclaiming their right to the thrones, a right which their supporters, the Jacobites, upheld. There was a Jacobite rising in support of King James in 1689; his son 'the Old Pretender' nearly took Scotland in 1715, but the Jacobite dream ended with the defeat of his grandson, Prince Charles Edward, 'Bonnie Prince Charlie', at the Battle of Culloden on 16 April 1746

Campbell (Ancient)

Clan Campbell has its heartland in Argyll. Historically it has been at odds with many of its neighbours, but the Campbells' main 'crime', has been a knack of being on the winning side in most conflicts. That, and an eye for a good marriage propelled them to a position of power second only to the king in the early 18th century, owning land from fertile Ayrshire up to Cawdor on the Moray Firth.

Inveraray Castle by Loch Fyne was rebuilt in 1744. The castle is still home for the Duke of Argyll.

problem of making estates pay was not restricted to incomers. Some Chiefs such as MacDonnell of Glengarry and the Duke of Sutherland were, for differing reasons, just as ruthless in clearing their lands.

Some Chiefs such as the Duke of Argyll, and Sir Ludovic Grant of Grant built new planned villages for their dispossessed tenants. Some like MacLeod of MacLeod ruined themselves in trying to provide some relief. One of the MacPherson lairds owned 5,000 acres in Pennsylvania and populated it with clansmen. The MacNab eventually emigrated himself with many of his clan.

However, as a result of this enforced diaspora, there are now Scots throughout the English-speaking world. Many more Highland gatherings are held in North America than in Scotland itself; clan societies preserve Highland cultural traditions and provide a focus for international friendship and for the exploration of genealogy. Happily, the clan system is alive and well in the third millennium.

PROSCRIPTION OF TARTAN

Tartan was considered to be a part of the rich Celtic cultural mix which inspired successive generations of Highlanders to attempt the restoration by force of the exiled Stewarts to the thrones of Scotland and England. After defeating the Highland army at the Battle of Culloden in 1746, the government acted decisively: the 'Disarming Act' banned the carrying of weapons, the wearing of Highland dress and the playing of bagpipes. Since a tartan plaid was the only dress that many clansmen possessed, the ban was hard and not universally respected, however no further reason was now needed to lock up or deport any tartan-clad Highlander who looked suspicious. The proscription on the wearing of tartan was lifted in 1782 on the insistence of the Marquis of Montrose.

Famous Clans

Clan Chattan is a confederation of clans, including amongst others, Davidsons, Shaws, MacPhersons, MacGillivrays, and traditionally led by the MacKintoshes. The original lands were at Torcastle near the foot of Loch Arkaig but under pressure from aggressive islanders, the Chiefs withdrew to Rothiemurchus in Strathspey, leaving a vacuum that was quickly filled by the Camerons. The resultant Cameron - Clan Chattan feud lasted for the next three hundred years. In the sixteenth century as punishment for a murder, the king deprived a Shaw Chief of his lands at Rothiemurchus and gave them to the Grants who still hold them.

The **Campbells** have their heartland in Argyll, and Inveraray Castle on Loch Fyne is still home to the Chief. This clan has historically been at odds with many of its

Gunns and Keiths

Clan Gunn, originally Vikings, had long controlled Caithness. The Keiths were incomers who acquired Ackergill Tower by marriage. For many months Helen Gunn, the 'Beauty of Braemore' had resisted the advances of Dugald Keith of Ackergill and when she married another, Dugald surrounded her father's house, carried her off to Ackergill and imprisoned her in an upstairs chamber. Rather than yield, Helen threw herself from the tower and a stone still marks the spot where she landed. The Gunns sought their revenge and eventually the two sides agreed to a decisive battle of champions: each side should attend with only twelve horses. Twelve mounted Gunn warriors duly arrived, however the Keiths chose a literal interpretation and appeared with two men on each horse. The slaughter included the Gunn Chief and four of his sons.

Dunvegan Castle in the north west of the Isle of Skye has been the stronghold of the Chiefs of Clan MacLeod for 800 years. Until 1745 it could only be accessed from the sea.

The Gunns descend from Vikings who crossed to Caithness in the 12th century.

Gunn (Ancient)

MacGregor (Modern)

The MacGregors, or 'Children of the Mist', were forced from their lands in Glenstrae, Glenorchy and Glenlochy by the expansionist Campbells. They retreated to the mountains and lived by preying on others, acquiring such a reputation as thieves and brigands that in 1603 the name of MacGregor was outlawed, meaning that just to own the name was punishable by death. The ban was lifted in 1774 and the MacGregors played a prominent role in the ceremonies surrounding George IV's visit to Scotland in 1822.

Immortalised in Sir Walter Scott's eponymous novel, Rob Roy MacGregor (opposite) was one of the leading cattle thieves and blackmailers in a society where success in such activities was much admired.

neighbours, and when a man by the name of Campbell was appointed Manager at the new Glencoe Visitor Centre in 2002, there were genuine protests from MacDonalds in the area. It was at Glencoe in 1692 that some members of Clan Campbell carried out, on government orders, a massacre of MacDonalds. The Campbells' main 'crime' however, has been a knack of being on the winning side in most conflicts. That, and an eye for a good marriage propelled these vassals of the MacDougall Lords of Lorne in 1296 to a position of power second only to the king in the early eighteenth century, owning land from fertile Ayrshire up to Cawdor on the Moray Firth.

Somerled, Lord of the Isles, whose grandson, Donald of Islay, is the progenitor of the **MacDonalds**, controlled the western seaboard and the islands in the mid 1150s. From that time until the close of the 15th century, the MacDonalds

FRASERS & MACDONALDS

In 1544, the Chiefship of the MacDonalds of Clanranald was in dispute. Lord Lovat, Chief of the Frasers championed the cause of his nephew who had lived at the Frasers' Castle Dounie. MacDonalds had been raiding Fraser lands and Lovat eagerly took four hundred men down by Loch Ness to Inverlochy, to be joined by a party of Gordons. His nephew was apparently installed as Chief, and the allies returned home separately. However a band of MacDonalds had been stalking the Fraser contingent and ambushed them at Blar-na-Leine 'the field of shirts', by Loch Lochy — so called later as it was a sweltering July day and every man discarded his heavy plaid. A bloody battle left only five Frasers and eight MacDonalds standing. Amongst the slain were Lord Lovat and his son.

CUNNINGHAMS & MONTGOMERYS

A Cunningham Earl was traditionally the 'Justiciar' dispensing justice in Ayrshire …until the surprise appointment of the Montgomery Chief. This prompted a Cunningham raid into Montgomery lands. Montgomerys then burnt the Cunninghams' Kerelaw Castle, prompting three Cunninghams to ambush and murder the Montgomery Chief. Two of these murderers were soon cut to pieces and every other Cunningham the Montgomerys could find was killed. But they missed a few, since the Montgomery Chief's seat of Eglinton Castle was subsequently burnt. And so it went on. Whilst such feuds were commonplace in the Highlands, James VI was so concerned by this lawlessness so close to his court that he summoned both sides on two occasions ordering that the killing should stop.

would constantly challenge the power of the Kings of Scotland, regularly attacking the king's castle at Urquhart on Loch Ness, disputing titles, and sacking Inverness for good measure. It was finally James IV who invaded the islands and stripped MacDonald of his title, granting the various branches of the clan – MacDonalds of Sleat, Clanranald and Glengarry – individual charters to their own lands and so dissipating the previous power of the clan.

The **MacGregors**, or 'Children of the Mist', with their lands in Glenstrae, Glenorchy and Glenlochy unfortunately stood in the way of the expansionist Campbells. Banished from their own lands they preyed on others and acquired such a reputation as thieves and brigands that in 1603 the name of MacGregor was outlawed, meaning that just to have the

The 'Old Man of Storr' is a spectacular basalt stack on the shoulder of The Storr Mountain in Trotternish on the Isle of Skye. The MacLeods and MacDonalds fought over possession of Trotternish for centuries, with the land changing hands many times.

MACLEODS & MACDONALDS

Northern Skye was originally Macleod territory, controlled from their fortress at Dunvegan. But young Donald Gorm 5th Chief of the MacDonalds of Sleat drove the MacLeods out of Trotternish and built himself a castle at Duntulm. The dispute rumbled on until an alliance was agreed: Donald Gorm took Margaret, the MacLeod sister of Rory Mor of Dunvegan, in a trial marriage (a custom known as hand-fasting). However the two betrothed did not get along and Margaret lost an eye in an accident. At the end of the hand-fast period, Donald Gorm sent her back to Dunvegan on a one-eyed horse, led by a one-eyed groom, followed by a one-eyed dog. This of course perpetuated the feud and Margaret's weeping ghost is said to haunt Duntulm Castle still.

name was punishable by death. Ironically Rob Roy MacGregor, the most famous son of the clan used his mother's name, Campbell. The ban was lifted in 1774 and the MacGregors played a prominent role in the ceremonies surrounding George IV's visit to Scotland in 1822.

The **MacKenzies** were originally vassals of the Lords of the Isles, but not particularly loyal ones, often siding with the king in long-running power struggles. The Mackenzies profited from the harnessing of MacDonald power and also absorbed MacLeod lands, so that their territories stretched from the Outer Hebrides in the west to the Black Isle, north of Inverness. They were fervent supporters of the exiled Stewarts, losing lands and title in 1715, but did not fight as a clan at the Battle of Culloden. The Clan

Chief was created Earl of Seaforth in 1623 but this line died out and the present Chief, the Earl of Cromarty lives at Castle Leod near Dingwall.

The name **Gordon** comes from a village in Berwickshire that was the first stop for a Norman knight whose offspring would become the dominant clan in north east Scotland. They acquired Strathbogie in Aberdeenshire from Robert the Bruce, and their power grew steadily with lands stretching across to Loch Ness. Gordon Chiefs consistently provided leadership to the Scots Catholics. They never embraced Celtic culture and traditions, but Gordon Highlanders became one of Scotland's finest infantry regiments. Ironically it was the Catholic Mary Queen of Scots who had to move against their unbridled power, defeating them at Corrichie in 1562.

GORDONS & FORBES

The Gordons of Aberdeenshire were both expansionist, and Catholic – traditional supporters of the Stewarts; the Forbes, a smaller clan, had totally opposite loyalties. A long and bitter series of tit-for-tat murders punctuated the 15th and 16th centuries. In one such, whilst the men were away, Gordons besieged and burnt a Forbes Castle killing Margaret Campbell, daughter-in-law of the Chief, together with twenty-seven family and retainers. Another involved the seven sons of Henry Gordon of Knock who were out cutting peat, apparently on Forbes land. The Forbes laird surprised and beheaded them, tying their heads to their peat spades. When the Gordon heard this, he fell down the stair of his own tower and was also killed. However the peat spade murderer was executed in his own house by Gordon of Abergeldie.

Balmoral Castle by the River Dee in Aberdeenshire was bought by Queen Victoria in 1852 and rebuilt, as seen here, in 1859. The Royal Family spends up to eight weeks at Balmoral in early autumn.

STAND FAST

TARTAN

Scotland without tartan is as unthinkable as Edinburgh without a castle. And yet it is unclear why this distinctive checked material took root in the Highlands rather than in any other part of the world where fleeces were sheared and women could spin and weave. The word is not Gaelic like 'clan', but probably comes from the Old French tiretaine, a type of heavy material of no particular colour.

The first known use of the word tartan in Scotland was in 1538 when King James V ordered 'Heland tartane' to make close fitting trousers then known as 'hose'. Like most Highland aristocrats, the king had his tartan tailored to fit – more flattering and more practical for riding than a kilt.

The clansman had a different priority: warmth. His clothing was traditionally made at home by women who produced a rectangular length of thick material, about five foot across by fifteen foot long. The cloth would be more akin to that of present day tweed rather than the brightly-coloured smooth material of the last two hundred years. This garment was known as a plaid, from the Gaelic *plaide*, blanket, and was used both for day wear and for sleeping.

To wear the plaid, a belt is laid on the ground, and the pleated material laid on top. The wearer lies down on the material, gathering it about his waist with the belt; the material below his waist falls, still

The Piper to the Laird of Grant (opposite), painted in 1714, is shown in full costume with an extravagant pipe banner. Castle Grant near Grantown-on-Spey is shown in the background.

These Highlander and Lowlander male and female figures illustrate John Speed's map of 'The Kingdome of Scotland', 1622.

An early illustration of the kilt. Mercenary Scots in Europe about 1620, probably from MacKay's Regiment, wear bonnets, tartan plaid and in one case tartan hose (stockings).

The name ancestor of Clan MacKay was probably Ethelred, eldest son of King Malcolm III and Abbot of Dunkeld. The clan was later given lands in the north west corner of Scotland through marriage.

MacKay (Ancient)

pleated, to his knees; the remainder is brought over his left shoulder to be fixed with a brooch to a coarse linen shirt, his only other garment. Hence the correct name: the belted plaid.

We do not know that much about the shirt the clansman wore, but clearly it was sometimes quite long: the Marquis of Montrose at the battle of Kilsyth issued orders that his Highland levies should lay aside their plaids and knot the tails of their shirts between their legs. Indeed it was not unusual for Highlanders to discard their heavy plaids, making it easier to charge and use the sword; but this was not a strategy for the faint-hearted, especially at Sheriffmuir in November 1715 with snow on the ground.

We do not know the colour of the earliest plaids, probably the same colour as the sheep's wool. However over the centuries, women took to dyeing the wool before it was spun. The greens came from local plants, browns from the bark or roots of trees, and the rarer pinks and purples from lichens and heather. Without chemicals such as iron or alum to fix the dyes, *mùn* ('matured' urine) was used as a fixative. The finished plaid would no doubt boast a beautiful range of delicate colours at first, but would soon become stained with the mud, blood, sweat and tears of daily wear.

Highlanders in belted plaids would have prompted curiosity in the streets of Edinburgh or Glasgow. Lowlanders were suspicious of this strange uncivilised garb, and some vestiges of this attitude remain today: a Lowland laird, was asked recently if his family had a tartan. "No, thank God" he replied, 'my ancestors were always able to afford trousers'.

But things were to change. In 1707, against the wishes of the vast majority of Scots, an Act of Union bound England and Scotland together as the United Kingdom. Tartan was adopted by some as a defiant symbol of national identity and was now more often seen outside the Highlands. Thus, almost by accident, tartan embarked on a shaky journey to its present position as a major national symbol.

Highland women started to pass on the textile patterns associated with their house or district. The proper number of threads for each line or check of the pattern was

Clan Weapons

The sword, often of excellent Spanish workmanship, was the clansman's chief weapon. It was either the older two-handed sword or 'claymore' as featured in the film 'Braveheart' or the more modern broadsword. Highland army successes in the Jacobite campaigns of the 18th century were largely due to the impact of the charge and the ferocity and skill of the swordsmanship. As defence he had the 'targe', a small leather and wood shield; if lacking a targe he would wind his plaid round his left forearm. Attached to his belt, or held behind the targe, was a large dagger, the dirk. Some also had a small *sgian dubh*, or black knife concealed in the plaid or else in a stocking. Latterly some had a musket or pistol which was fired when within range of the enemy and then discarded.

Dress Tartans (top left) were originally worn by ladies and are of lighter weight often with a white background. The colours for Hunting Tartans (top right) were designed for camouflage and the weight is heavier. 'Ancient' and 'modern' tartans are more recent terms and have less historical significance.

Gordon (Dress)

MacMillan (Hunting)

Malcolm (Ancient)

Grant (Modern)

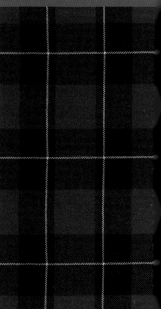

A knight from St Clare-sur-Elle in Normandy accompanied David I to Scotland and was given land at Rosslyn. A later Sinclair moved north, and built the cliff-top castles of Sinclair and Girnigoe in Caithness.

Sinclair (Modern Red)

The Edinburgh Military Tattoo (opposite), held in the first three weeks of August, is a stirring spectacle for Scot and visitor alike. Highland Games are held throughout the Highlands. The Braemar Gathering, (above), is one of the largest.

wound round the pattern stick in the correct order and the stick handed down from one generation to the next.

But none of this was recorded until in 1740 a Regiment of Highland Volunteers, later known as the Black Watch, was established and issued with a kilt of standard pattern in what became known as the Government Tartan. Interestingly, recruits were issued not just with the belted plaid but also with the *philabeg*, or modern kilt, being the lower part of the belted plaid with the pleats sewn in.

The convention of district patterns had by this time taken root and these no doubt came to be associated with the dominant clan. There were, however, few direct associations of patterns, known as 'setts', with particular names. An exception was Sir Ludovic Grant who issued instructions that all tenants must provide themselves with 'Highland coats, trews, and short hose of red and green tartan set broad-springed'. His son later added that gentlemen of his name must also wear whiskers. But sadly neither the broad-springed sett nor whiskers appears in any family portrait of the time.

There are numerous fine portraits of eighteenth-century clan Chiefs wearing the belted plaid. Since Chiefs were keen to

THE SURNAME MAC

Mac is quite simply the Gaelic word for son. Its use in a surname indicates a significant ancestor from whom subsequent generations take their name, thus Donald's offspring are known as MacDonald. The Mac prefix could also used to indicate a father's profession, such as MacSporran from *Mac an Sporain*, the sons of hereditary purse bearers to the Lords of the Isles.

Gordon is a village in Berwickshire that was first stop for a Norman knight whose descendants would become the dominant clan in north east Scotland. They acquired Strathbogie in Aberdeenshire from Robert the Bruce, and their power grew to influence events in Sutherland and by Loch Ness.

Gordon (Dress)

A piper plays in front of Borthwick Castle near Edinburgh where Mary Queen of Scots spent her last night with the Earl of Bothwell and next day escaped dressed as a servant boy.

show off the brightest and most expensive dyes when sitting for a portrait, these unfortunately give us little idea of what the simple clansmen wore. However they do tell us a little about the development of clan tartans. A painting, dated about 1750, of the two young sons of Lord MacDonald of Sleat shows four different tartans being worn. A painting of the eighteenth Thane of Cawdor in 1762 shows him wearing three different tartans, only one of which is a little like the present Campbell of Cawdor.

It is possible that the Chiefs had another plaid of local pattern to wear every day. But this would not be required as a form of clan uniform. Even as late as the Battle of Culloden in 1746, the clansman's identifying badge was a plant in his bonnet: heather for a MacDonald, bog myrtle for a Campbell; seaweed for MacNeil, holly for MacLean; yew for Fraser, whortleberry for Clan Chattan and bracken for Robertson.

Prince Charles Edward Stewart probably did not wear a kilt at Culloden – or indeed at any stage until he sought some anonymity when fleeing government troops after the battle. He probably wore red velvet breeches as he did when he rode into Edinburgh in 1745. Most of his army would have been wearing the belted plaid, but others would have worn the small kilt or philabeg, and most of the officers would have worn tartan hose. The most accurate representation of clansmen at Culloden is the contemporary painting by David Morier, (see page 15) who had Highland prisoners placed at his disposal for the purpose and so the accuracy is likely to be good. It is interesting both that men wear

The Highland attire of Robert Louis Stevenson, Scotland's renowned Victorian author of such classic books as Treasure Island, The Strange case of Dr Jekyll and Mr Hyde and Kidnapped.

A dirk with Cairngorm ornamentation and integral knife and fork. A much simpler dirk was traditionally slung on the Highlander's belt.

more than one tartan and that many of these are more red than green, so in those days at least there was no distinction between green-based 'hunting' tartans and lighter 'dress' tartans.

The proscription on the wearing of tartan, imposed after Culloden, was lifted in 1782. But by this time all but a few bold souls in the extreme north and west were wearing trousers and most hand looms had fallen into disrepair. After thirty-six years there was no widespread enthusiasm in the Highlands to revert to an old form of dress.

Some 40 years later, Sir Walter Scott, an incurable romantic, best known for his novels such as *Waverley* and *Rob Roy* had a yearning for what his son-in-law would later call the 'Celtification of Scotland'. It was thus inevitable that in 1822 when he

assumed responsibility for the visit of George IV to Scotland, the first by a reigning monarch since 1650, there would be plenty tartan about.

There was to be a ball – for which the instruction had gone out that 'no gentleman is to be allowed to appear in anything but the ancient Highland costume'. Indeed the king himself would don belted plaid and tartan stockings, velvet jacket, bonnet pierced with eagle feathers and basket-hilted broadsword.

It became convention that heads of family could now adopt their own 'clan tartan'. So Lowland gentlemen who would never previously have dreamed of wearing a scrap of tartan, started visiting the famous Wilson Brothers, Weavers of Bannockburn to decide on a suitable family tartan to wear for the royal visit. They also invested in broadswords, dirks and claw-

A leather sporran for day wear. In past times it was used for carrying oatmeal.

MacLeod (Modern)

Hallkirk Highland Games. Many of the 'heavy' events of the modern Highland games derive from the trials of strength and fitness devised to keep the clans' warrior elite occupied in the long summer evenings.

butted pistols to ensure that they presented the right image to His Majesty.

Had it not been for Sir Walter Scott, Highland dress might now be confined to fancy dress parties, and tartan to travelling rugs and military uniforms. But more was to come. Twenty-six years later Queen Victoria and Prince Albert astonished their English courtiers by purchasing Balmoral Castle in remote Aberdeenshire. The curtains, carpets and even some chair covers in the rebuilt castle were in tartan; kilts became normal daily wear and everybody was encouraged to take part in Highland Balls with the reels and country dances that the Queen loved so much.

With such royal interest in these matters, the Victorians quickly created a protocol for the wearing of Highland dress. Rules were produced on the 'right' to wear tradition-less tartans invented barely fifty years earlier. Highland dress had 'correct' accoutrements: 'waist belt, baldric with

crested buckles, claymore or broadsword, dirk, *sgian dubh*, a pistol (single-barrelled muzzle loading having ramrod attached), and powder horn suspended by silver chain worn on the right side having the mouthpiece to the front'. The traditional dress of the warrior Celt was thus taken to its pinnacle of finery by the same elite that had tried so hard to stamp it out just a hundred years earlier.

Kilts or tartan 'trews' are still generally worn at Highland Balls that have continued, little changed, since Victorian times although protocol is now more relaxed. The kilt is regularly in evidence at weddings and is the customary wear for Highland Gatherings and other traditional occasions. Each year new tartans are created for families, individuals, areas or towns to reinforce their identity. So, from uncertain origins, tartan is now well established as a living symbol of the entire Scottish nation.

Clan Chiefs Today

There are literally hundreds of Scottish clan names and family septs known around the world today. However, only a small proportion of them still have a known clan Chief, as recognised by the current regulations of the Court of the Lord Lyon. They are:

The Royal House	Dewar	Johnstone	MacKinnon	Nesbitt
Agnew	Drummond	Keith	MacKintosh	Nicholson
Anstruther	Dunbar	Kennedy	MacLaren	Ogilvy
Arbuthnott	Dundas	Kerr	MacLean	Ramsay
Barclay	Durie	Kincaid	MacLennan	Rattray
Borthwick	Eliott	Lamont	MacLeod	Riddell
Boyd	Erskine	Leask	MacMillan	Robertson
Boyle	Farquharson	Lennox	MacNab	Rollo
Brodie	Fergusson	Leslie	MacNaghten	Rose
Bruce	Forbes	Lindsay	MacNeacail	Ross
Buchan	Forsyth	Lockhart	MacNeil of Barra	Ruthven
Burnett	Fraser	Lumsden		Scott
Cameron	Fraser of Lovat	MacAlester	MacPherson	Scrymgeour
Campbell	Gayre	MacArthur	MacTavish	Semphill
Carmichael	Gordon	McBain	MacThomas	Shaw
Carnegie	Graham	MacDonald	Maitland	Sinclair
Cathcart	Grant	Macdonald of Clanranald	Makgill	Skene
Charteris	Grierson		Malcolm	Stirling
Clan Chattan	Guthrie	MacDonald of Sleat	Mar	Strange
Chisholm	Haig		Marjoribanks	Sutherland
Cochrane	Haldane	MacDonnell of Glengarry	Matheson	Swinton
Colquhoun	Hannay		Menzies	Trotter
Cranstoun	Hay	MacDougall	Moffat	Urquhart
Crichton	Henderson	MacDowall	Moncreiffe	Wallace
Cumming	Hunter	MacGregor	Montgomerie	Wedderburn
Darroch	Innes	MacIntyre	Morrison	Wemyss
Davidson	Irvine of Drum	Mackay	Munro	
	Jardine	MacKenzie	Murray	

Highland Dancing, originally restricted to men and a traditional celebration after a victory, is now a widely accepted art form and an essential part of every Highland Games.

The Stewarts were initially stewards of the Royal Household but became kings through the marriage of a Stewart to the daughter of Robert the Bruce. The direct Stewart line died out with Prince Charles Edward and his brother, but the present royal family still has Stewart blood, through the daughter of James VI, Elizabeth of Bohemia, 'The Winter Queen', whose grandson was George I. King George V referred to the Royal Stewart as 'my personal tartan' and it is now effectively the official tartan of the Royal House of Scotland.

Clans and Tartans Information

To find out more about Scottish Clans and Tartans, there is a wealth of information on the internet.

Most clans now have associations, which can be easily accessed. If you are not sure of your family's clan connection, there are many sites with information on how to trace your clan origins. The Scottish Genealogy Society has an informative site with links to many aspects of research.

The Scottish Genealogy Society
15 Victoria Terrace
Edinburgh
EH1 2JL
Tel: 0131 220 3677
www.scotsgenealogy.com

Although there is no official registry of Scottish clans, the Court of the Lord Lyon in Edinburgh lists the clans that have Chiefs. They also deal with all aspects of heraldry in Scotland. Burke's Peerage Landed Gentry also has information on the clan Chiefs and ancestral research.

Court of the Lord Lyon
HM New Register House
Edinburgh
EH1 3YT
www.heraldry-scotland.co.uk

Burke's Peerage
209 St John's Hill
London
SW11 1TH
www.burke's-peerage.com

Many Clans now have their own museums, again this information can be found by contacting your Clan Association or Society.

Isle of Barra

At the Scottish Tartan Museum in Keith visitors can discover their heritage with over 700 tartans on their database. There is also a display of Highland dress throughout the centuries.

Scottish Tartans Museum
Institute Hall, Mid Street
Keith AB55
Tel: 01542 888419
Open: April – November

The Scottish Tartan Society, a charity based at Cockenzie in East Lothian, has the recorded history and counted the threads of nearly 3,000 tartans. The Hall of Records at their headquarters contains a comprehensive library with a collection of tartan samples, original manuscripts, paintings, prints and maps.

The Scottish Tartans Society
The Cockenzie Centre
Cockenzie,
East Lothian
www.scottish-tartans-society.org

The Scottish Tartan Authority is another body with historical archives and information on Tartans.

The Scottish Tartan Authority
Fraser House
25 Commissioner Street
Crieff
PH7 3AY
Tel: 01764 655444
www.tartansauthority.com

The Tartan Weaving Mill and Exhibition is a working mill in Edinburgh's Old Town showing how tartan is produced along with guided tours and exhibits on the whole process from shearing sheep to the weaving of the cloth.

Tartan Weaving Mill and Exhibition
555 Castlehill, Royal Mile
Edinburgh
EH1 2ND
Tel: 0131 226 1555
www.tartanweavingmill.co.uk

First published in Great Britain in 2003 by
Colin Baxter Photography Ltd.,
Grantown-on-Spey
PH26 3NA, Scotland
www.colinbaxter.co.uk
Text by Alastair Cunningham
© Colin Baxter Photography Ltd. 2003

Photographs © by:
Colin Baxter: Pages 1, 4, 5, 6, 7, 8, 9, 12, 13, 16, 17, 20, 21, 26, 27.
Doug Corrance: Page 19. Fotomas Index: Page 24. Glasgow Museums: Page 11.
National Galleries of Scotland: Page 14. National Library of Scotland: Page 23.
National Museum of Scotland: Page 22. Wendy Price: Page 2: Map.
Glyn Satterley: Pages 28, 29, 30, 31, 32. The Royal Collection © Her
Majesty Queen Elizabeth II, Photograph by Antonia Reeve: Page 15.
Illustration © Jim Proudfoot: Page 10.

A CIP Catalogue record for this book is available
from the British Library.
ISBN 1-84107-172-2
Printed in China

Front Cover Photographs clockwise from left to right:
Piper to the Laird of Castle Grant © National Museum of Scotland.
Duart Castle, Isle of Mull © Colin Baxter.
Grave slab, Kildalton, Islay © Scotland in Focus.
Bonnie Prince Charlie © National Galleries of Scotland.
Braemar Highland Gathering © Colin Baxter.
Strathspey © Colin Baxter.
Back cover photograph *Blair Castle* © Colin Baxter

The author and publisher would like to thank the following people
for their kind assistance in the production of this book:
Roderick Balfour
Hector Russell Kiltmaker, Inverness
www.hector-russell.com
The Court of the Lord Lyon
John Paul Photography, Inverness